Jason Irwin

STOCK MARKET GUIDE FOR BEGINNERS 2021/2022:

STRATEGIES

The most complete guide to learn the best trading techniques & strategies to invest in the stock market

owned by the owners themselves, not affiliated with this document.

Table of Contents

INTRODUCTION 1

CHAPTER 1   INVESTMENT WINNING STRATEGIES.........................4

SCREENING TOOLS 4

    More About Screening.. 6

BROKERAGE ORDERS 8

INTERNATIONAL STOCK INVESTING 10

CHAPTER 2   BEST TECHNIQUES STRATEGIES AND TACTICS 12

    Stay Flexible... 12

    Commit to a Plan... 13

    Have Measured Expectations... 14

    Choose Personalized Strategies.. 15

    Be Disciplined 15

    Seek Absolute Truth... 16

    Focus On Logic... 17

STRATEGIES THAT WILL MAKE YOU SUCCESSFUL................................... 19

    Price Action Trading 19

    Buy and Hold 22

CHAPTER 3   INDICATORS...23

MOVING AVERAGES 25

    How to Use Moving Averages? 25

RSI 27

BOLLINGER BANDS 31

CHAPTER 4   MANAGE RISK..34

HIRE A STOCKBROKER 36

DEVELOP A TRADING PLAN 39

MAINTAIN SIMPLICITY... 41

ESTABLISH A STOP-LOSS LEVEL 43

DETERMINE YOUR POSITION SIZE.. 45

CURB YOUR EMOTIONS... 48

CHAPTER 5   TIME TESTED STRATEGIES THAT ACTUALLY WORK...............49

Back Test Every Strategy Before Implementation 51

STRATEGY 1: MOVING AVERAGE STRATEGY 52

Which MAVG Should You Use?.. 54

STRATEGY 2: CHANNELING STOCKS 55

STRATEGY 3: RSI—RELATIVE STRENGTH INDEX 57

STRATEGY 4: TRAILING STOP STRATEGY.................................. 59

CHAPTER 6   HOW AND WHEN YOU SHOULD BUY................................61

WHO DOES YOUR TRADING? 63

DISCOUNT BROKERS 65

Full-Service Brokers 65

HOW TO TRADE YOUR STOCKS? 69

READING A STOCK QUOTE 71

LIMITING YOUR TAXES 74

CHAPTER 7   KNOW THE IMPORTANCE OF TRADING STRATEGIES 75

HOW STRATEGIES IMPACT YOUR BOTTOM LINE 79

Always Focus on ROI (Return of Investment) 80

CONCLUSION 84

INTRODUCTION

To get the most out of your stock market activity you have to get to know it as if it were your best friend, you have to try to grasp its secrets and make them your own.

Once you've done that, most of the work is already done, after that you'll simply have to put into practice in a repetitive way what you've learned and, in the meantime, put in your pocket the income you've always dreamed of.

To get what you want most of all and to see your capital grow by leaps and bounds, all you have to do is apply stock market strategies.

The financial products you can find online to operate in the stock market and place your orders work great, and the strategies I will discuss here have been thoroughly studied to be effective when applied to the most important stock exchange assets.

What does "effective strategies" mean? Basically, they allow, if well used, to catch the right signals to intervene correctly in the financial markets. The stock market strategies I am going to talk about, placed in the right hands, and I hope they are yours, can change your life.

On the contrary, whoever decides not to use stock market strategies will not only never see a penny, but worse, will be forced to give up the money that was intended to be used as investment capital, because whoever does not use stock market strategies is destined to lose it, no matter what.

Many people know about stock market trading, and as many people would like to become traders thinking that it is an easy job, but very few people actually realize the real potential they have when they decide to start a career in the stock market.

Investing in the stock market is very convenient, but it is even more convenient when you decide to do it online through a qualified platform, where you are subject to much fewer rules and pressures and where you are therefore much more free in the management of your investment activity.

Believe me the problem here is not to understand if you can really earn on the stock market with strategies, but only if you are cut out to do it. There are those who start earning impressive amounts of money right away and then lose everything immediately by gambling money as a bet.

Then there are those who start and behave wisely like an ant, which works slowly for several months preparing to face the winter but then enjoying life thanks to the sacrifices made previously.

This is the focal point of exploiting stock market strategies. You too must do like the ant and not like the cicada. Money will be nothing but a consequence of this kind of serious and forward-looking approach to stock market trading.

But, remember well, without proper initial training you will go nowhere even with the best strategies explained in this book, but this is as true in the stock market as in any other existing activity.

If you think you have the right basis to approach trading with knowledge, then you are in the right place, indeed, in the right book!

CHAPTER 1 INVESTMENT WINNING STRATEGIES

Screening Tools

In the world of investments, screening is the process of assessing a potential investment with the intention of analyzing it according to certain criteria. The most common use is to reduce risks and manage costs when trading in financial markets. In general, screening can help investors diversify their portfolios by including only those stocks that meet certain criteria.

The idea is that if you hold too many shares in one company, your risk will be elevated significantly. In addition, if you are holding too many shares in companies that have very low trading volumes, your transaction costs will rise. This will reduce your profits and may even put your entire portfolio at high risk. Screening helps to avoid these issues.

Screening can be done by analyzing fundamental data, technical indicators, or both of these elements together. It is important to remember that every screening tool has a weakness and the combination of different tools is the best way to get an objective analysis of a stock or a substantial number of stocks.

Precision is very important when performing screening so that the final result is as accurate as possible. For example, when you are using fundamental data to screen stocks, it is important to make sure that the data you have gathered relates to the most current financial year. At times, small errors may be made when referring to historical data and these inaccuracies can impact your analysis.

Screening tools can be created manually or with the help of software such as Excel which will help to make the process quicker and more efficient.

The four most popular screening tools around today in the investment strategies world are GDP/GNP for International stocks, Dividend Yield for dividend-paying stocks, P/E and P/B mix for Growth stocks, and PEG ratio for Value stocks.

More About Screening

Screening is one of the most useful tools in trading and investing. It is used in many different kinds of investments and in different ways. It is based on using economic, or production, indicators to classify the potential performance of a stock and to identify overvalued or undervalued stocks. Some producers are more sensitive to market conditions than others; thus, they will have more volatility.

Screening helps investors to identify potentially profitable companies with declining risk and a consistent return on equity (ROE).

The following are some of the most important reasons why screening tools are used:

- Screening tools can help you to detect potential investments that would be suitable and profitable.

- A screening tool is based on a set of criteria. The most common are fundamental criteria.

- To establish an investment portfolio, you need to make sure that your stocks meet all the required financial ratios to ensure financial stability and profitability. By using screening tools, you will be able to filter them out automatically and save time.

Brokerage Orders

In a brokerage order, you can buy more than one kind of investment, such as stocks and bonds. Brokerage orders are also known as multiple orders. By entering multiple brokerage orders at once, you can trade on the markets without using the same type of transaction. Buying stocks with a purchase order and then shorting them with a sell order is one kind of brokerage orders.

Although these types of trades are not illegal, they may be considered market manipulation. If this type of behavior is suspected, the investigation begins by gathering information about the suspect's brokerage records; their portfolio holdings; and anything else that may reveal insider trading or other illegal activity.

When a brokerage order is entered, the market maker may be able to see that you have entered multiple orders. If they see that you are attempting to do something illegal, they will probably reject the order and call it off. This is why it is important that you enter your orders with a legitimate reason and an honest plan.

There are many kinds of brokerage orders, and some of them are proprietary (they belong to a particular brokerage firm). If the brokerage firm suspects that you are trading on public information, they may question why a trader from their firm would do something like that. In response, you should disclose any relevant information and explain that your orders were entered without knowledge of the specific prices of your holdings.

Strategies that actually work: Covered call options, put options, cash, EE saving bonds, I bond, Sector mutual funds, motif investing, bearish exchange-traded funds, dividend yield exchange-traded funds, consumer staples exchange-traded funds.

International Stock Investing

International stock investing is one of the most difficult things to do in the world. It is because of this, most people don't invest internationally. Instead, most people are still investing only in US stocks using different brokers and platforms.

But it's not all bad though, International trading offers the opportunity to invest at a higher risk level which can result in large returns over time.

One of the biggest advantages of international stock trading is that it offers the opportunity to diversify your portfolio, which can result in a lower overall risk. This is because different markets fluctuate differently from each other, giving you an opportunity to "diversify" the risk in your portfolio.

Many investors also believe there will be a better return on their investment if they invest internationally rather than investing at home because many foreign companies are still growing and offer good profitability potential, while US stocks have already reached their peak.

There are other advantages of international stock investing. For example, you can invest in foreign stocks without paying any extra fees. Many brokerages charge a commission every time you buy or sell a stock, but these commissions can add up if you're trading internationally. You can also take advantage of special promotions offered by brokers for trading with them—which means there is no monthly service charge and additional fees—and so you get more for your money when investing internationally.

The biggest disadvantage of international stock trading is that it's more complicated to do than at home. If you don't have any previous experience with foreign stocks, you'll need a good guide to help you learn the basics. You'll also need to spend a considerable amount of time doing research and learning about the companies you want to invest in.

CHAPTER 2 BEST TECHNIQUES STRATEGIES AND TACTICS

To succeed in stock markets, there are plans you need to master.

Stay Flexible

The stock market is a volatile place, which means that, if you ever hope to be successful when investing, then you need to remain ready to pivot at a moment's notice. The market can change in a matter of minutes, which means a stock on a long-running profitability streak can suddenly turn around and become worthless, literally overnight. This means that, if you want to succeed, you are going to need to limit the influence the past has on your decisions and instead focus on the information available in the present and what it will likely mean for the future. Be ready to ditch investments that are turning on you, and reevaluate previous choices if you hope to see reliable results in the long term.

Commit to a Plan

The plan that you create is going to be critical to your success in the long term, but only if you stick with it every time you choose an investment. While it won't lead you to success with every trade, if you create it using the proper criteria, then it should lead you to make profitable trades more than 50 percent of the time, which means you will succeed in the end as long as you stick with it religiously. Furthermore, knowing the acceptable criteria when it comes to selling and buying is crucial to ensure that you will be able to take advantage of emerging trends at a time when they will do you the best.

Have Measured Expectations

While it is possible to grow rich from investing in the stock market, it is challenging since this kind of growth doesn't happen overnight. Rather, most people who find success there slowly amass assets over time by holding on to profitable trades and getting rid of those that don't pan out before they can generate too much loss.

Additionally, it is likely to take you a prolonged period of time before you get the hang of things, which means you should expect to post a losing record for the first few months you start investing in stocks while you are learning the ropes. Note that this is normal; stick with it if you hope to eventually cross from the red into the black. Going into the process with a realistic idea of what it's going to take to be successful is an ideal way of ensuring that the learning curve will be as manageable as possible.

Choose Personalized Strategies

Just because you hear about a strategy that is guaranteed to work because someone else found success with it is no real indicator that it is going to work for you. While there is certainly no reason not to give it a try, it is important to ensure that it stands up to your standards and matches your natural investment inclinations as well. If it doesn't, the investment will be unlikely to generate the results you need.

Instead, it is always important to be on the lookout for new strategies that line up with your inclinations to use as a stepping stone to stock investing success as opposed to barriers that need to be circumvented to see any results. Remaining true to yourself is always going to be the most reliable way to see positive results in the long run.

Be Disciplined

It is common for many new traders to go after one type of stock simply because they have a gut feeling about it. The sad truth of the matter is that those gut feelings rarely if ever, payout effectively. As such, if you follow this scattershot approach, you are going to end up making it more difficult to turn a profit in both the short and long term. What's worse, if you do end up finding success with this process then all you will be learning is bad habits which will translate to fewer overall successes in the future. Instead of focusing on your gut, it is important to focus on building the discipline you need to make the right choices, even if your gut is telling you something else. While this will likely be hard at first, it will get easier with time.

Seek Absolute Truth

It doesn't matter if you feel that the price of a given stock is too low or too high, the only thing you can reliably focus on is its current price. If the facts say that a stock should be valued higher than it currently is, then you will want to buy, and if it is lower, then you will want to sell, end of the story. You need to remain impartial about these facts and simply do what they tell you. Developing an attachment to a given stock is only going to hurt your results in the long run.

Focus On Logic

After you have formed a successful plan, following it precisely with each trade that you make will always be the most logical next step. This means that, even if the trade doesn't end up working out the way you expected, you should still be pleased with yourself as long as you did what made the most sense at the moment. Going off the book is going to lead to failure far more often than it leads to success. Instead of raging against failed trades, simply look at them as the statistical balance to the other more profitable trades you are likely to make more than 50 percent of the time, assuming your plan is sound.

Sometimes doing nothing is the right choice: If you have reason to believe a specific stock is overvalued, then you will want to sell; if it is undervalued, then you will want to buy. The same principles go for when a stock is stuck in the middle of the road; the best action is to wait for a stronger signal to appear to indicate a movement in one direction or another. Many new traders find that waiting without making a move is one of the hardest things to do.

Making trades just to trade is always going to be folly. Be patient when the market is stagnant or moving at a faster rate. Wait until things normalize to enjoy reliable profits. Your goal should always be to make trades for the sake of profit, not just to trade for trading's sake.

Understand that there are no sure things: The odds of finding a system that will accurately predict trades 100 percent of the time, or even 90 percent of the time, are extremely small. In fact, you have a better chance of winning the lottery or being struck by lightning than of getting anywhere close to those numbers. There are just too many variables to consider at all times, even before you factor in chance and pure, dumb luck. Rather than wasting time looking for the impossible, you will find much better results by looking for a plan that you can rely on and just take the additional loss with a grain of salt.

Strategies That Will Make You Successful

Price Action Trading

At its most fundamental, price action trading can be thought of as a way for a trader to determine the current state of the market based on what it currently looks like, what any number of indicators say about it after the fact. This is a great strategy for those who are interested in getting started as quickly as possible, as you are only required to study the market in its current form. Additionally, focusing on just the price will make it easier to avoid much of the largely superfluous information that is circling the market causing static, which makes it more difficult to determine what is going on.

In order to determine when to trade using price action, you are going to need to use the trading platform that came with the brokerage you chose and utilize what is known as price bars. Price bars are a representation of price information over a specific time, broken down into weekly, daily, 1 hour, 30-minute, or 5-minute intervals. To create an accurate price bar, you need the open price for the given stock in the chosen time, the high for the time period, the low for the time period, and the closing price. With this data, you should end up with a box with a line through it. The line represents the high and the low for the day while the edges of the box show the opening and closing prices.

In addition to summarizing the information for the timeframe in question, it also provides relevant information for your purposes. This includes the range of the stock, which is a representation of how volatile the market currently is. The bigger the box in relation to the line, the more active and volatile the market currently is. The more volatile the market currently is; the more risk you undertake when making a move.

In addition to the range, consider the physical orientation of the box; if the close price is above the open price, then the market improved over the timeframe; if the close is below the open, then the market lost value. Take into account the size of the box as a whole. The bigger the box, the stronger the market is overall.

What this type of strategy provides you with is a clear idea of what the levels of resistance and support are like for the time period in question. This, in turn, allows you to pick trades with a higher degree of certainty. All you need to do is keep in mind that if demand is stronger than supply, the price is going to increase and vice versa. If the movement indicates that this is likely to continue in the same direction, then you will want to pick the point where it is likely to happen again and use that as your entry point. If the opposite is true, then you are going to want to sell ASAP to prevent yourself from losing out on gains you have already seen. If the price reaches the support level, then demand will exceed supply and if it reaches the resistance level then supply will exceed demand.

Buy and Hold

The buy and hold strategy is a type of passive investment in which, as the name implies, shareholders buy into a stock that has strong long-term potential and then hold onto it even when the markets see a downturn. This strategy looks to the efficient market to be a hypothesis for success, which states that it is impossible to see above-average returns when adjusting for risk. This means that it is never a good idea to resort to active trading. It also says that seeing decreases in value in the short term is fine as long as the long-term trend remains positive.

CHAPTER 3 INDICATORS

The primary tools of technical analysis are the candlestick charts and indicators. Being a successful trader is, to a certain extent, about odds. It's impossible for anyone to know the future. In addition, there can be unexpected events like a sudden news release. If that happens, you can ruin your trade in the blink of an eye.

So, while we can't predict the future with absolute certainty, what we can do is increase the probability of success. The main way to do that is to incorporate multiple indicators together with your candlestick analysis. And then you want to use your take profit and stop-loss orders to ensure that your trade isn't destroyed by some unexpected move, no matter the source.

Now it's important to realize that despite the large array of available tools, you don't necessarily improve your position by using a huge number of them simultaneously. In other words, the more tools that you're using, the less attention you are going to be paying to the signals each tool is giving you. It's better to master a small number of tools and indicators to become a better trader. If I were a new trader, I would much rather be an expert at candlesticks, which means understanding all the possible patterns inside and out, than I would want to be in a situation where my understanding of candlesticks is shallow and I'm throwing a whole bunch of indicators on my charts. In the same way, it's important to know that while there are several indicators available, they are usually giving you the same information. It's better to take two or three indicators and use them with the candlestick charts for your technical analysis.

Moving Averages

The first indicator that we are going to look at is called a moving average. To calculate a moving average, the system looks at a past number of prices called periods. Depending on your timeframe, that is what the period is going to be. If you're looking at five-minute intervals (i.e., five-minute trading sessions), one period is going to be a five-minute interval. Therefore, if you take a nine-period moving average, it will take the prices for the past nine five-minute intervals and then calculate the average. The default on most charting applications is to use the closing price for each trading session to calculate the averages.

How to Use Moving Averages?

The reason that we use moving averages is so that we can spot trend reversals. You will be using moving averages in conjunction with your candlestick analysis. A typical approach is to take a look at your candlestick charts and look for signs of a trend reversal, then you can check your moving averages and see if they confirm what the candlestick chart is telling you. However, trading platforms allow you to overlay moving averages on top of your charts. Hence, we can always have our moving averages on the chart so that we can look for the signals we seek in the candlesticks and the moving averages simultaneously. The more of a short-term trader that you are, the more important it is to be on top of the information. You need to move fast if you're a scalper or a day trader. The way that moving averages are used is to compare or utilize two moving averages with different periods on the same chart. One moving average will be a short period moving average. Typically, a nine-period moving average is used for the short period option. For a long period, you can use different values, such as a 20-period moving average. There may be reasons to use different time frames, we could use a 20-period moving average, together with a 50-period average. Some traders will even use 200-period moving averages in their analysis.

RSI

The next indicator we are going to look at is called the Relative Strength Index, or RSI. Many trading platforms have this on their charts by default. You use the Relative Strength indicator to determine whether a market is overbought or oversold. Let's explore what those terms mean.

If a market is oversold, that means too many people have sold their positions. In the case of a currency pair on Forex, this would mean that the secondary currency has gotten too to the primary currency. But you can still say it's an oversold signal because people are selling the currency pair to favor the secondary currency. The Relative Strength Index ranges between zero and 100. Be cut off, is usually used to indicate oversold conditions, which is when the Relative Strength Index drops below 30. If this happens and the market is oversold, it should indicate a coming trend reversal. At the very least, it would indicate that the prices are not going to continue dropping.

Therefore, if you had sold the currency pair because you thought the secondary would increase in proportion or against the primary, this would be a strong signal that you should buy back your position.

On the other hand, if you are interested in betting on the primary currency, oversold conditions could be a good signal to buy the currency pair. This would be done under the assumption that the overall trend would reverse and we would be soon witnessing an increase in prices.

The relative strength indicator is also used to look for overbought conditions. When financial security is overbought, this means we are expecting it has risen as far as it's going to go in price. Therefore, overbought conditions indicate that the price is going to start dropping in the near future.

For the relative strength indicator, if the value goes above 70, this is taken as a signal of overbought conditions. Let's look at how we would handle it.

First, let's consider the bullish investor. That is the trader has purchased the currency pair in anticipation that the base currency is going to rise in price. In this situation, if you see an RSI above 70, this could be an indicator that you should exit your position by selling the currency pair.

If you hadn't taken a position at all, you still would pay attention even if you were looking to bet on the base currency. Although it would be a little bit far off, this would draw your attention to the fact that prices are going to drop and so an opportunity to enter a position at a low price might be presenting itself in the near future.

Now we consider it is the opposite situation. This time you are betting on the secondary currency. In that case, an overbought situation is an opportunity to sell the currency pair. When a currency pair is overbought if you are looking for gains in the secondary currency that is an opportunity to enter your position.

People can get seduced by the RSI. They can also get seduced by the many other indicators that you can add to your charts. But it's important to take them all with a grain of salt. I hate to be repetitive, but this is very important. What this means is what we want to do is utilize the tools that are available to the fullest extent possible. But in every case, you want to confirm what the indicator is telling you before you act.

Bollinger Bands

The last major indicator that we are going to consider is called Bollinger bands. This is a very powerful indicator, especially when prices are bouncing around in between a limited range. Bollinger bands give you three pieces of information. The first is a 20-period moving average. This is going to form a central line within the bands. The bottom band is going to be defined by a low-price level which is calculated to be two standard deviations below the mean. You can think of the bottom band as defining the level of price supports at any given time. When you're going to use price supports as a factor in deciding when to trade, where to put your stop-loss, or where to take profits, this is a good way to do it without relying on your analysis of the charts.

The second band is found above the moving average. This is also calculated to be two standard deviations above the mean. Therefore, you can take this to be resistance. Then, this would be the upper pricing level that you would expect shortly. Again, it can be used in the way you would use resistance. Therefore, it can be used to define points to enter or exit trades. It would be also used for a take-profit pricing level if you are buying a currency pair, or setting a stop loss for those that are selling the currency pair.

People also use the relative positions of the candlesticks with respect to the Bollinger bands to determine price reversals. You will look for candlesticks touching levels of support and resistance that is looking for the candlesticks to touch outside Bollinger bands. If you see the candlesticks touching the upper Bollinger band and sometimes they will even go outside of it that could be a signal of a coming price reversal heading downwards.

Conversely, if you see the candlesticks touching the lower Bollinger band curve, or going below it, that can also be a signal of importance. In this case, it would indicate a coming rise in prices.

Bollinger bands are one of the more advanced indicators available. As you can see, it's providing you three things in one. As such, the information that I've just given you tends to be fairly accurate. You should also note that Bollinger bands can also be set up using different metrics. When you add a Bollinger band to your charts, you have choices about which moving average to use. You can also determine how many standard deviations to use for the upper and lower curves. The default is to use a 20-period moving average in most cases, together with two standard deviations. There are good reasons to use this approach. Over short time periods, although there can certainly be big price moves, it's relatively unlikely that prices are going to be following outside of the two standard deviation range. Using three standard deviations would be far too lenient.

And conversely, using one standard deviation would be extremely conservative. Maybe if you were scalping, one standard deviation could be a consideration so that you could take profit on small price moves. At the same time, it might constrain you too much so that you are taking profit at levels that are too small to overcome the spread.

CHAPTER 4 MANAGE RISK

Both account and risk management exercises are activities that coincide as you go through the Day Trading investment cycle. It is very important for you to ensure that you achieve your aims of making significant profits, while at the same time, mitigating losses from the capital in which you invested.

Managing your account and the risks associated with Day Trading involves the responsible handling of the available equity in your brokerage account. You can perform account management through further investment in profitable stocks, ingenious trade maneuverability, or exiting from trade deals that stagnate.

On the other hand, your risk management strategies involve responding appropriately to alleviate prospective losses in an uncertain future and limiting the degree of your exposure to financial risks. The following are some of the primary strategies that you can apply to your Day Trading to ensure active risk and account management.

Hire a Stockbroker

As a beginner or a new investor participating in Day Trading, it could turn challenging if you went at it alone. You need advice on the right stock opportunities in which to invest, guidelines on how to handle probable financial risk exposures, and knowledge of technical analysis to keep track of your capital progress.

A qualified and registered stockbroker typically offers these financial services at a commission or flat fee. You need to seek the assistance of such stockbrokers to tap into their experience and expertise in Day Trading. Besides, the chances of attaining your profitable goals increase when you employ the services of a stockbroker.

Account management and risk management are strategies that are innate to a stockbroker, especially when given access to the account. Therefore, you need to open a brokerage account from which all your Day Trading activities take place. Maintaining liquidity in this account is as essential as making the right trade deals.

Since you may not interact with the stock market all the time, running the trading account becomes the responsibility of your stockbroker. You need to give him or her freedom to make informed choices on long and short trades, however risky they might seem at first. Trust your broker to understand what he or she is doing with the account and hence the need to hire an honest stockbroker, preferably from a well-known brokerage firm.

In addition, it is usual for your stockbroker to have extensive experience with managing financial risks. Most of the strategies meant to combat potential financial threats such as spreads are somewhat complex to understand, let alone apply them effectively. The same levels of complications and fair sophistication apply to the tools used for technical analyses.

You need to follow these analytic tools to make informed choices based on their data. A stockbroker comes in handy at this point to assist in data interpretation. You also get to learn about the various management strategies of which you had no idea previously. Generally, account and risk management in Day Trading is often all about making the correct decisions from technical analysis.

Develop a Trading Plan

This document is a crucial tool for you as a new investor in Day Trading. If you do not possess such a program, then it may be time to develop one that tailors to your specific trading. Creating a trading plan is an activity that you need to perform with the help of your stockbroker. The broker typically has experience in the Day Trading sector, and so he or she can offer you pointers on the trading opportunities that have the potential of being productive. Based on this vital tip, you can create a comprehensive trading plan that contains an overall objective that is set out. Besides, the program should have tactical or short-term goals set at regular intervals during the cycle. The primary purpose of these operational targets is to enable you to keep track of the progress of your Day Trading activities.

Once you complete the creation of a trading plan, you must stick to its guidelines at all times. You and your broker need to have a chance at Day Trading's success. Hence, you both have to adhere to the rules of the trading plan. It sets out instructions on how you should react and what measures to take with your capital under different situations. Since the

39

future of Day Trading is often uncertain, it is essential for your plan to cover emergency financial responses. If you diligently adhere to your trading plan, your likelihood of attaining profitable returns eventually increases significantly. In addition, you will have a policy of intervention to potentially risky financial exposures.

Maintain Simplicity

In Day Trading, you may falsely believe that you need to overextend yourself on high-risk investments to make substantial amounts of return. This belief is a dangerous position for you to adopt when getting into Day Trading. Keep in mind the notion that the underlying stocks are often a more volatile type of security than other investments. Fluctuations in the value of the traded stock are frequent and typically occur over a relatively short period.

You must learn how to make small trade deals on the stock from the low-risk end of the trading spectrum. Beware of succumbing to the desire to stick your neck out for the riskier stocks. Greed and emotional influence are the leading causes of such irresponsible trading practices. In the case of a specific trade deal turning awful, you need to exercise restraint from the urge to make illogical trading decisions to try to cover your previous loss.

Besides, keep an eye out for volatile stocks and avoid trading in them as much as possible. If you can, distance yourself and your portfolio from such stocks. Ask your broker to let go of highly fluctuating stocks entirely due to their corresponding high levels of financial risk. All these missteps are easily avoidable when you stick to the simple trading practices laid out in your trading plan.

As a result, you will evade massive losses associated with complicated, high-risk trading that is subject to a high level of emotional influence. Proper and responsible account management demands that you avoid rash decisions that may lead to prospective losses and missing out on potential profits. Risk management also takes care of itself by minimizing your exposure to the high-risk end of the trading spectrum and keeping clear of volatile stocks.

Establish a Stop-Loss Level

To manage the amount of risk to which you are willing to expose your trading portfolio, you can issue orders that reverse potentially hurtful financial positions. A stop-loss order limits the amount of stock price that you can tolerate without taking a significant financial hit.

This order enables your stockbroker to cease all the Day Trading activities immediately. It allows him or her to instantly stop either buying or selling any further stocks based on the unfavorable prices. The order indicates the specific stock price beyond which you cannot risk either purchasing or offloading, respectively, because doing so would expose you to an apparent financial loss.

Getting into an apparent losing situation is an irresponsible practice on your part. Eventually, you will end up with a depleted brokerage account due to the mismanagement of the available capital that you previously had. Stop-loss orders are especially useful when conducting Day Trading on volatile stocks. It is advisable to set the stop-loss order to an amount that is as close as possible to your trading entry point.

Besides, close monitoring of the fluctuating price of your particular stock is a must to ensure the successful execution of the order when required. As you can realize, when used in this manner on volatile stocks, such stop-loss orders act as risk management tools that mitigate the financial downside associated with rapidly fluctuating stocks.

Determine Your Position Size

Position sizing involves making decisions on the amount of capital with which you intend to take part in particular day trade. The size of your investment is directly proportional to the level of risk exposure. A high-volume trade will invariably expose you to more financial risks than a small number of trade deals.

Your brokerage account will often get caught in the crosshairs of high-risk transactions and Day Trading practices. Exhaustion of the amount of available capital in your trading account becomes even more likely. Therefore, an early determination of your trading position is essential before engaging in any form of transaction. Your position size divides into an account and trade risk based on the number of shares of stock that you acquire on a particular trade.

For you to minimize any potential financial downfall resulting from the degree of your account risk, you must set a limit on the amount of capital to trade in each deal or transaction. A fixed ratio or small percentage is often the recommended format for this account limit. Maintaining consistency is vital in setting these account restrictions.

Do not keep altering the allocated portion for different trading deals. You should pick one value and apply it to all of your transactions during the Day Trading. A preferable limit should be one percent of your available capital balance or less. Make sure to adhere to the strategy of simplicity by making only small amounts of capital allocations to the low-risk stocks.

In addition to the risks to your trading account, the other financial exposure from position sizing concerns the trade risk. The best strategy to counteract trade risk involves the use of stop-loss orders. The gap between the entry point to your Day Trading and the specific numerical amount set as the limit on the order constitutes your trade risk. As earlier mentioned, this order enables you or your stockbroker to exit from a trade deal upon reaching the set limit of loss. This action results in capping further loss of capital; hence, it contributes to managing financial risk in this manner.

Consequently, you should execute stop-loss orders close to your trading entry point to minimize the likelihood of potential losses spiraling out of control. Be careful not to set it excessively tight to inhibit your ability to carry out any trading. Position sizing is responsible for both account and risk management. The evasive maneuvers described usually contribute towards minimizing risk.

Remember to allow for some flexibility when setting the restriction value on a stop-loss order. You need this leeway to give your stocks a chance to increase in value without encountering an obstacle in the form of the stop-loss order. Such moves enable you to maintain a healthy trading account. The number of shares needed for a potentially profitable trade relates to your ideal position size, as shown below.

The ideal number of shares required (Position Size) = Account risk / Trade risk.

Curb Your Emotions

Emotional influence on Day Trading practices can turn counterproductive very fast if you are not careful. The primary emotions to look out for are self-confidence and fear. Excessive confidence can cause you to have a false sense of self-belief in your trading abilities. As a result, you may end up making illogical trading choices and decisions based on your cockiness.

You should understand that you become more prone to develop a false sense of overconfidence whenever you are on a winning streak.

CHAPTER 5   TIME TESTED STRATEGIES THAT ACTUALLY WORK

All advance investors apply various strategies to their portfolios. Like a magician, most investors won't share their secret tricks of the trait, until of course, it's not a secret anymore. I can't say I have a magic formula or a secret sauce. However, I've been trading for 30 years, and along with my mistakes, I also learned some strategies through just trial and error.

In my sincere attempt to take you from novice to advance investor in one book, I like to introduce some of the basic, yet powerful strategies that can make a huge difference in your investments. We will keep most of these strategies straightforward and basics, but powerful.

Back Test Every Strategy Before Implementation

Back-test simply means go back in the past (1yr, 2yrs, 5yrs, 10yrs, how back in the past depends on how long in the future you would like to hold this security. Is it a quick in/out, or are you planning on holding this for a while?) And to see how often you would have made/lost money applying this strategy. Some strategies work great on some stock but not on others, so back-test it.

If you went back 1 year, invested $1,000, and implemented a strategy, and realized you would have been right 3 times and wrong 1 time and you would have made $200. Then you can go back 2yrs, 5yrs, 10yrs and see how you would have done. If you backtested and the results are positive, then you can attempt to introduce that strategy into that security. Remember not all strategies work on all security & there are no guarantees; the minute you apply a strategy and it doesn't work, back-test again to make sure it's still the best strategy available. Therefore, it's pertinent that you back-test with enough data, to ensure that the odds are definitely in your favor!

Strategy 1: Moving Average Strategy

One of the most used and most effective strategies is the moving average (MAVG).

This strategy is used to gauge the direction of the trend. Moving average, averages out series of market close and plots them. For example, a 10-day MAVG will take the last 10 closes and averages them out, and plots them. Therefore, if the market is moving up, the average of closes will also rise.

Once you plot the MAVG, if the trend of the stock is moving up the MAVG will also be moving up but will be below the stock price rising steadily under the stock price. If the stock price is trending down, you will see the MAVG above the stock price falling with the stock price.

Go ahead, plot a moving average and look! This is the best way to learn!

Magic happens when the stock price and MAVG cross each other, this signifies a change of a trend. Thus, in this strategy, one would buy and hold a stock as long as MAVG is below the stock price, and when the stock price crosses

MAVG and MAVG is now above the stock, one would sell as this signifies a downward trend!

Contrary when the stock crosses the MAVG and starts to climb above the MAVG, this would signify a buy signal.

In this strategy, you would look for a cross of MAVG with stock price and buy/sell on this signal over and over. You would rinse/repeat.

Below is a chart of CMI from 3/2015 to 12/2017 with a 100-day MAVG. I would sell as the price goes below MAVG and buy as the price comes above MAVG.

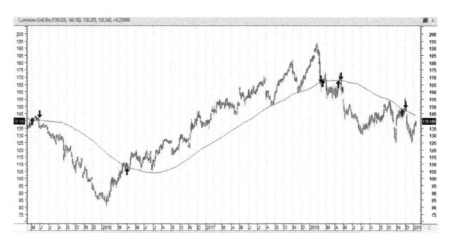

The most common MAVG plots are for 10-day, 20-day, 25-day, 50-day, 100-day, and 200-day.

Which MAVG Should You Use?

You can try a few of them and back-test to see if any fit the chart, sometimes it's trial and error.

Typically, you would use 10-day MAVG for short-term investing and 200-day MAVG for long-term investing i.e. retirement account. Also, note that the nature of every stock is also different. Some stocks are more volatile (move up/down quickly) and if you use shorter MAVG it will give more buy/sell signal, you may not want to go in and out of position during market volatility. The best way to figure out which MAVG is right is to do back-testing. Look how many times you would have won/lost and how much you would have profited using a 10-day, 50-day MAVG.

Strategy 2: Channeling Stocks

No matter how much research you do, some stocks just titter-totter! For example, if you had purchased "HALL" on Jan 1, 2016, around $11.75 and held on to it until Dec. 31st, 2017, its worth at $10.25. There would be no major win or loss. If I bought and held this stock, I would not have made any money.

You can see within this timeframe, the stock reached $11.50 at least 7 times and it reached $10.25 at least 7 times. What if I bought it for around $10.25 and sold it at $11.50 seven times?

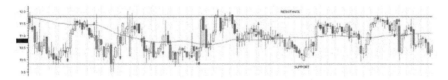

In this strategy, you would find stocks such as these and continue to buy and sell them at a price interval. I've done this for the last 2yrs on this stock. You would find the resistance and support and buy and sell them repeatedly.

You would probably not want to be too greedy by waiting for the stock to come all the way down or all the way up, you want most touches at resistance and support. To prevent further loss, you may want to have another deep support in case the stock turns on you and gets out of the channeling pattern.

There are some stocks that are just not buy-and-hold stocks. Don't fight them, just look at the chart, if you noticed these patterns, don't think that because you bought them, and you did your research they are going to shoot for the moon. For example, if you look at AT&T "T," in early 2000 the stock was worth approx. $40, and end of 2017 the stock is worth about $40. Last 18 years there has been so much news, so many rumors, etc., don't fight the chart, even if this stock rises to $100, there are many good performers out there, don't fight 20 years of history. In defense of "T," this may not be completely accurate since "T" is known to provide great dividends, but nonetheless, dividends can be taken away at any time the company decides to.

Strategy 3: RSI—Relative Strength Index

RSI is usually plotted for 14 days, with two horizontal lines at 20 and 80. A buy signal would be generated when RSI crosses the oversold line (20). The sell signal is generated when RSI crosses the overbought line (80).

In this indicator, you really do need to pick the right stock. Some stocks appear to stay above or below the line for quite a while. When stocks do this, they are either on a down or uptrend, in that case, this is not the best indicator to use. Other stocks remain between 20-80, these stocks don't give clear overbought or oversold conditions. Ideally, you would want to see stocks with spikes above or below the lines and drop back down. This may be stated rather simplistic, and in my experience, you can't rely on this unless you have back-tested (as with any of the other strategies, but especially this one). This strategy does not work well with many stocks. This may be a good secondary strategy, if you are on the fence about getting in/out, and you need some additional reassurance, consider RSI and see if it's below 20 or above 80, and then back-test to see if it has been reliable.

In this example, I'm using BRKb, with 35/70 RSI. I am putting an order to sell anytime RSI reaches above 70 and will buy when RSI reaches below 35. My buy orders are more accurate than my sell order. Many times, after I sold a stock it continues to rise. In this case, I can possibly buy the stock when it reaches below 35 but use another indicator to sell. Red lines show the RSI is less than 35 and will be buying and the blue line indicates I will be selling. You may get multiple buy signals and multiple sell signals, therefore don't sell all your holdings at once but sell them in batches. If you have 300 shares, sell 100 each time.

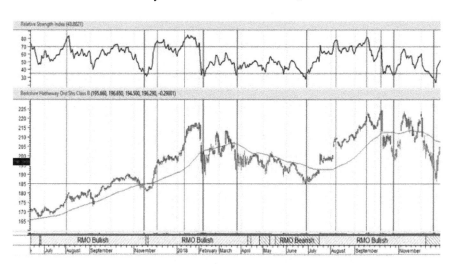

Strategy 4: Trailing Stop Strategy

Prevent your losses and lock in your profits!

This strategy works well with stocks that are momentum/trendy stocks. Stocks that tend to show you a diagonal line up are ideally the best ones. Once you have made some money in the stock, this strategy will secure your profit and ensure you won't lose but gaining all upside potential if the stock goes up. Here is how the strategy works.

Once you are in the position (you own the stock). And the stock has risen, you will place a stop loss below the fluctuation of the stock and/or below the previous support. The stock naturally fluctuates, it doesn't go straight up or straight down, it moves in a zig-zag (fluctuation). You want to put a stop-loss order below the fluctuation and below the previous support, this will give the stock some chance to fluctuate without you being sold out! If the stock changes trend and begins to dive on you, your stop-loss order gets activated and your stock is sold (making whatever profit you have made thus far on the stock or if you just bought it, you may have some loss based on the risk you were willing to take). If the stock goes up, you are still in the position and now you will cancel the old order and move the stop-loss order up, locking in your profit!

Let's say you did your homework first and found a momentum stock with a diagonal chart, of course, there is no guarantee the charts will continue their trend up, but we are going to assume it's going to continue what it has done in the past. You see chart for 'MA' appears to fit that model. So, you buy 'MA" for around $100 in September 2016. You will then place your stop loss below the last support, which is around $94 (where the horizontal line is placed). If the stock goes below $94, your trade will get executed and you will sell the stock for a loss of $6! Therefore, that is your risk, you will never lose more than $6 per share in this example and you must be willing to take that risk. However, if the stock goes up (as we predict based on the prior historical chart) you will be raising the stop loss, locking in the profit until the stock goes below your stop-loss order.

CHAPTER 6 HOW AND WHEN YOU SHOULD BUY

You've done the tough part. Choosing stocks—without a doubt the most crucial piece of the equity-investing procedure—requires more time, effort, and belief than any other part of the job. Your responsibilities don't end there. In fact, they didn't even begin with a stock choice. Consider stock picking as picking a route on the journey to monetary freedom, understanding that the route will frequently alter to accommodate the detours and weather dangers that are market changes.

Who Does Your Trading?

Have you ever asked the question, "So how can I find an excellent broker and not somebody who will jet off to the Cayman Islands on my dime?" The word "broker" doesn't accurately fill individuals with self-confidence, and great deals of individuals have captivated that thought, primarily because a few brokers have certainly absconded with investors' funds. Reasonably, if you use a standard brokerage home, you need not stress about money a thief's permanent vacation.

The Securities Investor Protection Corporation (SIPC) works to assist financiers harmed by misaligned brokers, claiming to have returned properties to 99% of financiers qualified for protection. The SIPC doesn't help you recover your losses if you buy the wrong stocks and lose your shirt. Simply put, if you get scammed or suckered into a lousy financial investment, that's your issue. But if a broker takes your cash or loses it in the process of doing something illegal or dishonest, that's the SIPC's problem.

Do not lose sleep over a broker taking your cash. Instead, focus on picking the right stocks, and focus on what kind of broker to utilize.

Discount Brokers

The name states it all. Discount brokers, such as TD Ameritrade, E * Trade, Charles Schwab, or Scottrade, buy and offer stocks on behalf of financiers at lower commissions. However, they likewise provide no direct financial investment guidance. While the four listed above represent a few of the best-known discount brokers, lots of others offer online trading services for less than $10 per transaction. If you choose to make trades by telephone, anticipate paying a higher commission. For many investors who want to evaluate and select their stocks or act on advice from a third-party specialist, such as a newsletter, a discount broker will do the trick.

Full-Service Brokers

On top of making trades for you, full-service brokers may likewise provide guidance or carry out other services. A full-service broker may make sense if you look for stock recommendations or your monetary situation requires customized assistance. Be prepared to pay a lot more for your trades—in some cases $50 per transaction or more.

To compare brokers, simply visit their sites and sneak around. Processing stock transactions have ended up being a product company, indicating practically all the companies do it well. When you research study brokers, search for features relevant to you, such as:

- Lots of brokers offer discount rates for accounts above $25,000 or $100,000, but low rollers don't get special treatment, and all brokers need minimum balances for accounts. If you prepare to start a little, make sure your broker can accommodate you.

- Site style. Each broker website includes its own user interface. You'll discover some more user-friendly than others, and the ones you choose may not interest someone else. Rely less on advice from others and more on your individual when it comes to navigating a broker's website

- Volume discounts. If you prepare to make many trades (which, as a novice, you most likely should not), some brokers lower their charges for regular traders.

- Variety of securities. All brokers sell stocks and ETFs. Shop around if you prepare to buy conventional mutual funds. Some brokers provide a lot of shared funds readily available for no transaction charge; however, the choice and costs differ considerably from firm to company.

- Research services. Some discount rate brokers offer access to online tools, stock screeners, and research study reports. A couple of likewise let clients interact in online neighborhoods where investors share concepts.

If you'd rather prevent brokers altogether, you can purchase stocks straight from the business that released them (or straight from the transfer agent the business employs). Dividend reinvestment plans (DRIPs) permit financiers to acquire stocks without a broker.

Getting that very first stock in your name isn't too hard. More than 1,000 U.S. businesses offer DRIP plans, and about 600 of them enable you to acquire even your very first share through the strategy. At the same time, when you acquire stock through a broker, it ultimately comes from you. Because the broker has custody of the shares, they are held in the brokerage company's name generally described as the street name—for ease of buying, selling, and transferring. Rather than letting the broker utilize its street name, you can pay to sign up the shares in your name and have the physical certificate sent out to you. You can then utilize those shares to join DRIP strategies.

If your holdings in a stock trading at $50 per share pay a $5 dividend, you can acquire and reinvest the dividend 0.1 shares of the stock. The capability to gradually add funds to multiple stocks over time appeals to investors who don't have much cash; however, they do plan to set aside cash for financial investment regularly.

DRIPs attract investors who seek to construct wealth slowly and who don't plan to trade often. Because many little stocks (and many big ones) do not provide the plans, DRIP financiers enjoy fewer choices. Of course, for numerous investors, 1,000 stocks still seem like lots of selection.

How to Trade Your Stocks?

For the most part, novices ought to buy and sell their stocks at a prevailing rate. Before you make a deal online, visit your broker's website and click on the trading link. The site will ask you the number of shares you wish to buy, and whether you want to make a market order or a limit order.

The broker will make the buy at the best available price when you put in a market order to purchase 50 shares of Acme Widget. It should not matter much whether you purchase at $39 or $41 if you've analyzed Acme Widget and like the stock at $40 per share.

Limit orders, on the other hand, are for financiers who wish to buy or offer just if the share price reaches a specific level. For instance, if you consider Acme too expensive at $40 however, would purchase it at $35, you can submit a limitation order with a $35 rate, and the broker will purchase the shares if they dip to $35 or below. Limitation orders offer greater control over the price paid for a stock; however, they can keep investors out of stock. If Acme drops to $35.01, then rises to $50, the investor with the $35 limit order will never purchase the stock—and never share in the gains.

A limitation order to offer at $45 will get you out of stock at a price no lower than $45, as long as the stock rises to the target level before the order ends. Brokers usually charge higher commissions on limit orders than on market orders.

Reading a Stock Quote

You'll see a page with a lot of numbers when you open up a financial site and type in your ticker. While each website creates its pages differently, you can depend on seeing the majority of this information:

- Ask cost: The lowest cost a seller is prepared to accept for a security. For many large, heavily traded stocks, the quote and ask price will be close together. For thinly traded stocks, the bid-ask spread can get broad.

- Quote price: The highest rate a purchaser wants to spend on security. At any offered time, brokers handle millions of buy and sell orders, some of which suggest a particular rate to purchase or sell.

- Current cost: This number shows the most recent deal price, though totally free sites usually run on a delay, so their numbers are somewhat obsoleted.

- Day's variety: The low and high prices in the present days trading.

71

- Fifty-two-week range: The low and high costs over the last year.

- Volume: The number of shares traded.

Last, note that if you access a quote page after the market closes, you'll see end-of-day numbers. You'll discover intraday numbers if you visit throughout trading hours.

Some financiers choose to utilize stop orders—that develop into market orders after the stock hits a threshold. For instance, Acme trades at $40. You're scared it will fall hard, so you put in a stop order at $35. If the shares dip listed below $35, the stop order triggers and your broker sells the stock at the prevailing cost.

Stop orders have limits. You'll sell at about that cost if bad news breaks and the stock right away dips to $30 per share. A sell limitation order won't guarantee you a sale at $35, simply which you'll offer the shares at the going rate once the rate dips below $35.

Investors who use stop orders likewise run the danger of purchasing or selling stocks simply because the market rotates. Suppose you set a stop order at 10% below the stock's current cost to protect against unsightly losses because you fear the business will lose a patent suit that could cost it countless dollars in sales. What if the marketplace falls 15% and your stock slides with the rest of them? No lawsuit has emerged, and the factors you purchased the stock stay intact. The stop order would have offered you out of stock, which probably stands an excellent opportunity of recuperating when the market restores its momentum.

Put, limit orders permit you to enter into stocks if they fall or get out of stocks if they rise. Limit orders allow you to leave stocks if they fall or get into stocks if they increase. Your broker will offer you lots of trading alternatives beyond market, limitation, and stop orders. As you acquire experience, do not hesitate to broaden your horizons and explore brand-new methods to trade. But whatever you do, no matter your trading objectives, never forget the single essential trading guideline: If you do not comprehend how the trade works and why it makes sense, don't make the trade.

Limiting Your Taxes

Just a fool makes financial investment decisions without thinking about the tax ramifications. On the flip side of that coin, only a fool permits tax issues to become the chief driver of those same decisions. Since they don't want to pay taxes on the gains, far too many investors decline to sell stocks at earnings. When the scenario changes, and it no longer makes sense to hold the stock, failing to offer might cost them.

CHAPTER 7   KNOW THE IMPORTANCE OF TRADING STRATEGIES

Now that you have a clear idea about the terms involved in stock trading, as well as a clear idea of your risk appetite and risk profile, we can then talk about trading strategies. As the old saying goes, "If you fail to plan, you are actually planning to fail." This cannot be any truer than when applied to stock trading. How bad can it get? Well, you can lose thousands, if not, hundreds of thousands of dollars if you do not have a clear, well-thought-out strategy.

Think of your strategy as both a map and a compass. It is too easy to get into trading and just do everything by impulse. You let your emotions get the better of you. You get swept in by all sorts of trading fads and heavily hyped stock alerts that are "a sure thing."

Well, let me tell you if somebody could tell you how the market will trade tomorrow or at any point in the future, everybody would be a millionaire because those kinds of claims are a dime a dozen. It seems like everybody makes those claims, and unfortunately, individual traders have a very tough time making a living of stock trading because of these conflicting messages. They get all excited about a particular investment newsletter, and then they try it out; it does not pan out, subsequently, they get excited about another investment system, and on and on it goes. At the end of that journey, you have very little to show for all the time, effort, and yes, money you invested in stock trading.

It is important to begin trading stock with a strategy in mind. In other words, before you even begin trading your first penny's worth of stock, you have to have a strategy in place. Does this mean that you are wedded to the strategy for life? Absolutely not!

What this means, however, is that you at least are going to be trading in a systematic and methodical way. You are going to be trading with your eyes wide open and paying attention to all sorts of different factors. You are aware of the process; instead of just rushing from one hot stock or one trending stock to the other without really a clear idea of what you are doing and what your purpose is.

When you implement the different strategies that I outline below, you are essentially setting a map for yourself. Some people are looking for quick returns. They want to make thousands of dollars every single day. They want to make stock trading their livelihood. There are certain strategies that fit those needs.

Other people are looking simply to fight inflation. They just want to make sure that the money that they worked so hard to earn all these years maintains its value. There is a trading strategy for that.

For all other points in between, you have to focus on what your needs are and also your risk profile and appetite. Everything has to square with the particular trading strategy that you are using. For example, if you are in your 60s, it is probably a bad idea to get into day trading. You can lose your shirt and unlike a person who is in her early 20s, you most likely will not have as much time to get that money back. You cannot earn that money back because you are almost a few years away from retirement, or you have already retired.

You always have to factor in your risk profile as well as your risk appetite along with your needs. Sure, everybody can appreciate making several thousand dollars a day. Who would not? The problem is we may not have the proper profile for the strategies that give us a shot at making that kind of money through trading stocks. So, it is really important at this stage when selecting among different strategies to focus on how much capital you have, what year needs are, as well as your risk profile and appetite.

How Strategies Impact your Bottom Line

Your choice of strategy plays a big role in how you measure success. A day trader, for example, can call it a victory if he or she walks away with a $500 to $1,000-dollar gain every single day. That is a big deal to the day trader. Other people are looking for something more long-term. The success they see for themselves is buying Apple at $100 per share and selling it at $250 a share. The strategy you select impacts how you measure your success.

Always Focus on ROI (Return of Investment)

Let me let you in on a secret. The first trading strategy that you are going to implement when you start trading is probably not going to be the strategy that you are going to stick to in the long run.. Why? This is a learning process. What seemed like a good fit, in the beginning, might not be all that applicable? Something that may have seemed wild to you or something that does not fit your profile might be the better choice. Unfortunately, the only way to figure out which strategy is best for you is really to try one strategy after the other.

How do you know when it is time to switch out from one strategy to an alternative one? Very simple. Keep a laser focus on your ROI. Pay attention to the amount of time you put into trading as well as your actual profits.

ROI is calculated both in terms of overall gains (this is the profit that you make) and the time involved. You are always going to divide the profit by the amount of time. This is your adjusted ROI factoring in time. Think of it this way. It is really easy to get excited when you hear that somebody made 100% ROI. In other words, they invested 10,000, and they got 20,000. Sounds awesome, right? What is not to love, right?

Well, what if it took them 30 years to get that return? That is ridiculous! That is ridiculously low compared to other ROI you could have otherwise enjoyed pursuing other investment opportunities in the stock market. Do you see how this works? You could have adopted a trading strategy and blown away that ROI over that ridiculously long period of time.

Let ROI be your North Star or guiding light when it comes to figuring out the best stock trading strategy. Again, the strategy that may seem so appealing right now may not practically be a good idea. Similarly, an investment strategy that may seem quite risky or may seem a bit too technical for you may be the strategy that you would do best with. You will only know once you implement.

Your job right now is quite simple. Know when to quit a strategy and switch to a new one. We are not talking about making thousands upon thousands of dollars a day. We are not talking about striking it rich and buying yourself a new Ferrari.

Our ambition is pretty straightforward and very limited yet realistic and positions you for great success in the future. The bottom line is you should focus on learning right now while minimizing your losses. Make no mistake about it, if you do not know what you are doing, the learning process can be a very expensive experience.

Your job right now is to learn as quickly as possible. Put simply, learn how to fail hastily at a minimal cost. This is important because a lot of people get all excited about figuring out what to do. The way life turns out is that you can also focus on learning what not to do. They both lead you to the same place. So, do yourself a big favor and either fail quickly but cheaply or be very clear on what you are looking for and pay attention to what you are doing and your return on investment, so you can eventually adopt the right trading strategy for you.

That's exactly what you do when you buy a mutual fund. Every mutual fund has a manager or a set of managers.

These people are professionals. These people know the financial industry. They've been around the block in terms of making the right calls, as far as stock purchases are concerned. They have a fairly good idea of when to buy and when to sell.

Still, despite their expertise, keep in mind that mutual funds have different rates of returns. Some mutual funds appreciate quite well. We're talking over 15% annual growth. Other mutual funds barely keep up with the annual rate of appreciation of the Dow Jones Industrial Average or major indexes. Others, unfortunately, underperform. Their rate of return is either negative or several points below the Dow Jones Industrial Average.

You have to use the Dow Jones Industrial Average as your basic metric because if you were to not do any research at all and just take your dollars and invest it in an index fund, that's the return you'll be getting. So, this should be your benchmark as far as mutual funds are concerned. That is the rate of return that the fund manager is trying to beat.

CONCLUSION

Thank you so much for making it to the end.

I hope that what was explained was useful to you and will be useful to you in the future.

Now you just have to put into practice the tips and techniques I have explained, maybe keeping this book handy whenever you have a doubt or feel confused.

The right strategies can really make the difference between a successful trader and one destined, alas, to failure.

As I have stressed several times during the narration, all those who do not use a forward-looking approach in investing in the stock market and who are not accustomed to study, and who do not plan wisely making this complex discipline a real mantra, well, they will not go very far.

But I am sure you will do great!

Lightning Source UK Ltd.
Milton Keynes UK
UKHW020617290722
406558UK00001B/12

9 781914 599705